Please Return
to
Ruby Hobenstod

TO TOUCH THE SKY

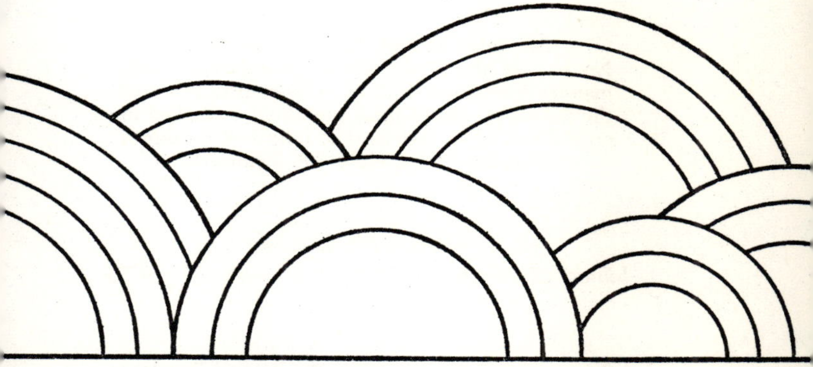

TO TOUCH THE SKY

June Parker Goldman

ABINGDON PRESS NASHVILLE AND NEW YORK

TO TOUCH THE SKY

ISBN 0-687-42310-4
Library of Congress Catalog Card Number: 70-84723

SET UP, PRINTED, AND BOUND BY THE PARTHENON PRESS, AT NASHVILLE, TENNESSEE, UNITED STATES OF AMERICA

DEDICATED WITH LOVE

To my parents
—who first set the sky in my heart

To my husband
—who filled it with stars

and

To my children
—who are the reason for having a sky

PREFACE

When a small child draws a landscape, he invariably leaves a band of white between the ground and the sky. He leaves this space because his sphere of knowledge is still too limited for him to know that earth and sky meet at the horizon. But he will learn.

Sometimes, when a Christian draws the landscape of his life, he also leaves a gap between earth and sky—but he leaves it because he can't quite believe that the things of God can intermingle with the things of man.

In a day when the gap between earth and sky seems wider than ever, the seeking Christian must move out of smallness toward a truer horizon where his faith can touch all that he does and all that he is.

Today's Christian has the exciting privilege of carrying a piece of the sky—and planting it in his little patch of earth—that the things of heaven and the things of earth might someday more nearly combine to become the kingdom of God.

Continually at work throughout the varied experiences of our lives there is an alchemy from which we distill a philosophy, a reason for being that becomes uniquely ours.

Looking back on my childhood and my early adult years, I am gratefully aware of the rather unusual circumstances that have shaped my life.

My childhood was spent, for the most part, in Japan, where my father was professor of English in what was known as a boys' higher school. He had come to Japan from New England, fresh out of college and full of ideals; he had quickly fallen in love with a charming and self-reliant Japanese secretary who soon became his wife—and later became my mother.

My father and mother and I lived in a modest but pleasant house in one of the suburbs of the large metropolitan port city of Kobe. Our house was nestled against the Kobe hills and overlooked the harbor. The view from my bedroom window always had something new to offer, as the seasons changed and as the large ships came and went. The sea was a partner in my dreams; and the sky, stretching to the farthest horizon beyond the breakwater, always gave me a reassuring sense of continuity.

The sea brought me to America in my middle teens, and I finished high school in a picturesque New England town in western Massachusetts. There, as in Kobe, I lived among the hills. But in the Berkshires there was no sea—except the sea of color that inundated the countryside every year in early October.

Memories of those years pile deep in my heart, like New England snow in New England valleys: the high school years during the turbulence of the Second World War; the poignant commencement program in which sixty-three chairs were left vacant in honor of the members of our graduating class who were already serving in the armed forces; the anguish of knowing that my father was being held in a prison camp in Japan, and the further anguish of not knowing what had happened to my mother; then the indescribable joy of our reunion when my parents were brought back to the United States in the first exchange of prisoners of war. The whole gamut of emotions was traveled during those years, and almost everything I had known changed—except the sky.

College brought new disciplines and new happiness, and the end of my senior year came more quickly than I had expected. But it marked more of a beginning than an ending, for soon after graduation I married a young seminary student; and I felt that the sky was not wide enough to contain my joy.

The days were always full: the busy routine of working while my husband finished seminary; the excitement of having our first baby, and the equal excitement and joy which attended the arrival of our second child, and our third; the anticipation of being assigned to our first parish, and the same happy anticipation of being assigned to all the other parishes that have followed.

Very early in my husband's ministry I learned how magnificent people are—and also how mediocre; but mostly I discovered how desperately people need one another—and need God. I learned, too, the redemptive quality of laughter; and I also discovered that a problem doesn't seem as large when viewed over a cup of coffee.

But I also learned something else—the limiting stereotype of "the minister's wife"; and very early I decided that stereotypes were not for me. I knew that every parishioner we would ever have would carry a definite image of the role I should play, and that each of these mental pictures would be different from every other. And so, intuitively, I decided to be myself.

Opportunities within each local parish have always been challenging; and equally fulfilling have been the opportunities that have taken me far beyond the local parish. And I keep discovering that whether I'm teaching a Sunday school class, or addressing an out-of-state convention, or cooking supper for my family, there are certain common denominators that human beings share. So I write this book, not with my pen but with my heart, hoping that some of these common yearnings may stand in bold relief against the sky.

CONTENTS

CENTAUR IN THE SPACE AGE

The twentieth century is known by many names: the Machine Age, the Atomic Age, the Space Age, and the Age of Technology, to list a few. We are living in a time so different from any other that the sociologist and the historian and the scientist all have been led to observe that man is becoming obsolete.

The computer has freed man from his cumbersome toil, we are told. He need no longer pick his way painstakingly through the raw materials of his inner resources. And we are reminded that it used to be such a plodding pilgrimage. However, I cannot help thinking that at least it was a pilgrimage.

When man grappled with life on the elemental level of ABC, he used his whole being—his heart and nerve and sinew—to move out of his cave, to carve out a wilderness, to unshackle his bonds, and to build his altar. Now, because so many of his former tasks are being done for him, man is finding it more and more difficult to make use of his whole being. And so the twentieth century has spawned the half-man, the computerized centaur that paws the earth with his pent-up frustrations.

To be fair we must admit that every age in history has had its half-men: the slave masters in the age of the pharaohs, the spectators at the Roman arenas, the tormentors of the Spanish Inquisition, the witch hunters at Salem, the storm troopers of the Nazi regime. These were the centaurs of their century; they were half man and half beast, and they were all half mad.

Today we are developing a new breed of centaur—half man and half machine, stilted, stifled, and sterile. It is a temptation for today's man to become suspicious and cynical as he sees the unfolding of strange new systems of thought and behavior.

Lest there be any misunderstanding, we need to acknowledge that technology is not bad in and of itself. In fact, man's very life depends heavily on technological advancement. We fear for man only at the point at which his technology may threaten to subjugate his humanness.

Two thousand years ago man was struggling under another tyranny. There were other idols to which he was sacrificing the essence of his humanity. And at that juncture in history, God sent a Messenger to reclaim man, to give him a feeling of value, and to lift him back up to the highest level of his humanness.

Because of the impact of that ministry of reconciliation and renewal, we, too, may take heart. But, like the step that had to be taken by the men Christ restored, our first step must be to rekindle in man the spark of the divine and to convince him of his intrinsic worth and the supreme value of his soul.

If we believe in the mission of the Messenger, then in spite of the fast-moving technology that surrounds us we may still celebrate one another's humanity and experience the joy of transmitting to and receiving from one another the spark of the divine.

Such an experience was mine not long ago, and it happened as surprisingly as spring!

My husband and I, together with my parents, had had the pleasure of planning a short vacation trip together. We decided that in spite of the fact that our time was going to be very brief, we would go to Expo '67 and see as much as possible in a day and a half. We hurried from one island to another, hoping to see a cross section of the fair. But the hours must have been jet-propelled, for all too soon we found ourselves with only one hour left. We decided that of the many exhibits we had not yet seen, the Russian Pavilion was one we surely shouldn't miss, for we knew that our friends back home would be asking many questions about it.

As soon as we entered that pavilion we realized that it would be impossible even to begin to see it if the four of us tried to stay together. So we parted company, agreeing to meet near the entrance at a given time.

I began my expedition through the vast exhibit hall; and the more I saw, the more depressed I became. To be sure, there were astonishing displays of man's technological progress, but everything seemed to convey the impression of being sleek and metallic, cold and impersonal. Nothing I saw gave me even a suggestion of warmth; and I longed to see something, anything, that might have in it the quality of humanness. But everywhere I looked there were only pistons and generators, levers and giant gears, and what seemed like acres of stainless steel.

And then, suddenly, I saw it—over in a small section of arts and crafts: a magnificent carving! It was of a simple peasant mother, seated on a low stool and balancing her small son on one foot, preparing to give him a ride. Whoever had made the carving had captured a universal theme, for every mother the world over has joggled her child on her foot.

The lines of the carving were fluid, forming a circular composition. The wood of the little boy's foot blended with the wood of the mother's, and his hands also merged into hers. The carving was called simply "The First Flight." It was so beautiful and struck such a responsive chord at the very center of my being that I felt compelled to express my joy to someone connected with the pavilion.

I remembered having seen a young man in uniform seated at a desk near the entrance.

Making my way there, I asked the young official if he spoke English. He nodded "no." Then, beckoning to another young man in uniform who was standing near the desk, he explained to me in halting and heavily accented words, "Sasha, he speak English."

I looked up at the tall young man who had joined us, and I said excitedly, "I would like to tell you what I think is the most beautiful and meaningful exhibit in your pavilion."

"Oh?" he asked. "What ees that?" And he gave me a look that added, "And who are *you* to tell *me* what is the best thing in my pavilion?"

"Well," I said, gathering up my courage, "I think that by far the most beautiful and significant thing in this entire pavilion is 'The First Flight,' the carving of the mother and child."

I watched the young man's face as he tried to focus his memory on the carving. And then, remembering it, he smiled broadly. "Yes—eet ees!" he agreed enthusiastically.

Suddenly, for just a moment, there was no geography between us, only the neighborhood of the heart. For, spanning the gulf between two separate ideologies, there was —for an instant—a bridge over which both of us could cross. And I shall always be grateful for that moment because, fleeting though it may have been, it held a hint of sunrise.

Perhaps underneath the brittle, calculating technology and all the false veneer of both cultures there was a common humanity, after all. "The First Flight" had brought a glimmer of hope, like the first streak of dawn in the sky!

THE WINGS OF THE SPIRIT

For many people there is a sense of finality in the events of today. My son is nineteen. He is waiting impatiently, but uncertainly, to come on stage to speak his lines. His uncertainty stems from not knowing whether he will have a chance to play his part before the final curtain comes down.

In such an age as this, the church should be center stage. That it isn't there is due either to the fact that it doesn't want to be or that society won't let it. We are surfeited with diatribes about the ills of the church. Everyone who is avant-garde, or who would like to be considered so, seems to be parroting the refrain, "The church is irrelevant." And the chorus is getting just a little tiresome.

True, there is a hungering and a thirsting today such as man has never felt before. But we might well ask, Is man thirsty—or bloodthirsty?

Often when man is angry with himself, he turns that anger upon the object of his love. By hurting what he loves he punishes himself, and this makes his anger bearable.

Could it be that the current attack against the church is a last, desperate expression of man's disaffection for himself? Does it assuage man's anger to say that the thing he has loved for a long time is now irrelevant?

In an age that is parched for answers, what could be more relevant than the invitation that is offered—"Ho, every one that thirsteth . . ."?

Every man who has tasted of the living water holds within his cup the compelling desire to share it. And every person who has partaken of some portion of Christ's love feels the urgency to pass it on. No one can give what he does not have himself. Each is able to transfer to another's life only what has been real in his own. So do we offer only the tenderness we have experienced, the forgiveness we have received, the laughter we have enjoyed, and the love we have been given.

It is not enough anymore simply to "keep the faith." We must convey it. But we convey best what we covet for others to know.

It is surprising how early in life this principle becomes operative. I hadn't realized it until the night that my youngest child lost her second tooth, an event which precipitated a happy discovery.

Now when the *first* tooth came out, everything had gone according to plan. My daughter had put the pearly little tooth under her pillow, as she had seen her brother and sister do when they had lost theirs, and then she had fallen asleep in complete confidence that the "good fairy" would come in the night and leave a dime in exchange for the tooth. Of course, my husband and I saw to it that the dime was where it should be before we went to bed that night. It was an excited child who found the anticipated coin under her pillow the next morning.

But the metamorphosis of tooth to coin

was not so easy to engineer the second time. The tooth came out just at bedtime on a night when the family finances were at a low ebb; as a matter of fact, they had ebbed entirely away, for it was the last day of the month! What was I going to do? The tooth had been placed expectantly under the pillow.

After the prayers were said, I went downstairs to do the dishes and to try to formulate some plan of action. I was so deep in thought that I didn't realize my son had come downstairs until he was standing beside me. He was holding the piggy bank he had received a few weeks earlier on his tenth birthday. Offering it to me, he asked, "Mommy, do you need a dime?"

I looked at him in wonder and puzzlement.

Sensing my surprise, he continued, "I heard you tell the paper boy today that you didn't have a speck of change, so I figured you might be needing a dime for tonight." He paused a moment; then, with his eyes twinkling he added, "Y'see, I know you're the good fairy; but let's keep it a secret for Jennifer."

My heart grew wings as I gathered my ten-year-old in my arms and promised him that this would be our special secret. This was the beginning of wisdom for my son and for me. For through his tender little offering, I had been able to verify a feeling I had had for some time but which had remained on the edge of my mind. Now I understood fully that when something is important for us, it is imperative to share it—else we perish.

For my son the idea of the good fairy was terribly important. And although from the vantage point of his ten years he had already evolved a somewhat more sophisticated interpretation of the good fairy concept, he still believed it was a very necessary part of his little sister's experience.

At ten he had taken his first tentative flight with the wings of the spirit. And because of the nature of the flight, I felt I could hope, with some assurance, that he would never confuse the idea of the good fairy with his concept of God. And I could also hope that as his wings grew stronger he would venture farther, and that his discoveries of God would propel him to share the joy of his faith with those who had not yet tried the sky.

FROM A PAIR OF BOOTS

The receding value of the individual may well be due to a current paradox: on the one hand, there is the growing power of the mob, the ever-increasing influence of group action, and the consequent pressure to conform to the group; on the other hand, there is the revolt against conformity, but a revolt that is led primarily by the asocial, amoral rebel rather than the thinker or the idealist. As a consequence, the word "individuality" has almost become synonymous with "peculiarity," with the result that any genuine individual effort is held suspect.

It is small wonder, then, that we are hearing more and more of such phrases as peer group, power bloc, mass media, group dynamics, and organization man. Individuality, in a positive and creative sense, has practically relinquished its place in the sun.

If there is to be a rebuttal on behalf of the individual, we must begin with a basic premise. And quite often we need look no farther than the mind of a child to find such a premise. For truly, children are in some respects the world's greatest philosophers; and without a doubt they are the most disarming.

When my two older children were preschoolers, they were playing one day in the driveway. Stuart was wearing a pair of brand-new cowboy boots. His sister, two years younger, had inherited his old boots. While the children were engrossed in play, their baby-sitter happened to come by on her way home from school. As she passed, she noticed the shiny boots; she stopped a minute to compliment Stuart on his proud new possession. Then, thinking that Candace might feel a bit left out with her hand-me-downs, she said, "Pretty soon you'll be able to have Stuart's shiny new boots too!"

"No," answered my four-year-old wistfully. "They'll have to small down."

Immediately her brother corrected her with, "No, Candace, *you'll* have to big up!"

The ability to "big up" is a tall order (if we may pun a little). In the enchanting story of *Alice in Wonderland,* Alice is able to grow smaller or taller at will, by alternately drinking the contents of a mysterious bottle and eating a tiny cake all beautifully decorated with currants. But we are not Alice. And fortunate it is that we are not; for if growing tall were as simple a matter as Alice found it to be, the world would soon be populated by a race of giants. However, physical proportions by themselves are no measure of a man's true height; for the stature of a man's soul is a more accurate yardstick of how tall a man really is.

Many years ago my father was one of fifty Americans in a Japanese prison camp. He made many discoveries during this experience, the primary one being that in prison men are stripped of all the superficial trappings they have depended on under normal conditions and the essence of each man stands out either as sham or as sterling.

Early in their internment, the men were confronted with an extremely difficult decision to make. Singapore had fallen to the Japanese army, and the nation was jubilant. At the prison camp the Americans were told that they would have to march in a victory parade and that there would be the added humiliation of having to wave Japanese flags by way of tribute.

The night before the parade the men debated the choice before them. They knew that if they marched in the victory celebration they would be betraying their conscience, their country, and their God. Yet they were well aware that if they refused to march, they might be punished severely or even put to death. The men discussed the pros and cons; they joined in the fellowship of prayer; they took ballot after ballot to determine what course they should follow. All night they deliberated. Finally, about dawn, they reached a decision. They had voted, down to the last man, that they would refuse to march in the victory parade and that they would take whatever consequences might follow.

About midmorning, when some of the prison guards came to distribute the flags which were to be carried, the spokesman for the prisoners stepped forward and stated simply that the men were not going to march in the parade. There was great consternation among the guards, who retreated to the prison office to confer with some higher officials. Then, just before the victory march was to begin, the prisoners were told curtly that they would not have to take part. This was a temporary relief for the men; but they didn't know what sort of retaliation might be taken against them after the parade or the next day or even the following week.

But nothing happened until four months later. Then, just before the men were to leave Japan on the first exchange of prisoners of war, a dinner was given in their honor. Unusual? Very! But that is what happened.

On this unique occasion the food was rather poor and the speeches equally so, but there was one deeply moving thing about the evening. Every Japanese official who spoke made reference to that day in February when fifty men, armed only with the courage of their convictions, had said, "No, we will not march in your parade!" Then it was explained to the men that theirs was the only camp in which none of the prisoners had been mistreated during their internment, the only prison camp from which all were able to walk out under their own power.

That was an evening the men never forgot. Nor did they forget the reason for it.

Fifty men, one interminable February night, had learned to "big up"; and the height to which they climbed had attracted the admiration of men who were their enemies. These fifty men had made the ultimate discovery that the growth of the inner man is a process, not of whittling *down,* but of whittling *off* the protective veneer that hides the real self from the scrutiny of other people and the even more penetrating gaze of God.

The individual Christian has the greatest possible challenge that is offered to man; for being an individual is difficult and demanding, and being a Christian is even more so. But to be both an individual and a Christian requires the maximum growth potential of which a person is capable.

To lift—to comfort—to share—to sacrifice—to gladden—to hope—to kneel: these are the verbs of growing.

Perhaps it is permissible to think, without being sacrilegious, that if Christ were giving his great commission today, he might say to us, "Grow ye, therefore—and then go!"

OUR HAMSTER HUMANITY

Growth is mandatory if one is to survive in our carnivorous culture. We are easily consumed, wholly or in part, if we are not big enough. And here the word "big" refers, not to the type of bigness that is associated with large corporations or a man's waist measurement, but rather to the size of his inner being.

Conflicting interests compete for our time; conflicting loyalties undermine our stability; creeds in conflict make inroads upon our faith; and the unceasing drive for material gain keeps us in continual conflict with our better selves.

Competition is paradoxical: it can be the starting gun of progress, and it can also be the death knell of integrity. The devastating nature of competition, when it is raw and unharnessed, came into shocking focus for me through an incident which will always remain indelibly etched on my mind.

It happened when my son was in his early teens. He had gone through all the usual phases of collecting stamps, looking for rocks, building model cars and planes, and raising guppies. Next in the natural progression of boys' hobbies came the hamster-raising stage; and I must admit that the entire family was properly grateful that hamsters had been chosen instead of white mice or snakes.

There had been two hamsters in the cage for several weeks, and they had been getting along together famously. Then the decision was made to add a third one. The old adage "three's a crowd" came to mind, and I expressed my concern to my son. But he was operating on the principle of "the more the merrier."

Two or three nights after the new arrival

had joined the original occupants of the hamster cage, one of my daughters made a startling discovery on her way to bed. She had stopped by to say good-night to the furry little creatures, but when she looked into their cage, she let out a horrified cry.

We all rushed to see what was the matter, but we were not prepared for what we saw: two of the hamsters were crouching in the back of the cage—and there, between them, was what was left of the third one!

Stunned by this turn of events I tried to shield the children from the grisly sight, but they had already seen it. I groped for something to say, but before I could find any words, my son observed, "Hamsters are just like people, aren't they? They eat each other up!" His indictment was almost more shocking than the tragedy in the hamster cage. I wanted to push it out of my mind, but my son's words kept dogging my thoughts so persistently that I finally had to do some serious thinking about the complexities of present-day competition.

What happens in a highly competitive society? Is competition the only reason for man's destructive tendencies, or are there other factors which lead to our social, political, and economic cannibalism? In what way do people eat each other up? Or should we pose a slightly different question —rather than being consumed by one another, as my son had charged, are we perhaps more often gobbled up by the circumstances in which we find ourselves?

We are at a point in history when more and more people are being swallowed up by events. Not long ago there was a heartbreaking story about a policeman in one of the southern states who had become a hero in the midst of an outbreak of violence in his city. He had acted calmly; his had been the one strong voice of reason that had quelled the unrest and brought it under control. But soon after the trouble had subsided and life had settled back to normal, his son was convicted of a break-in. It wasn't a serious burglary, but a break-in nevertheless. The father could not bear the shame that came to him and his wife; unable to cope with the fact that his son had betrayed his teaching and his trust, the father took his own life. It was a shattering experience for the entire community.

Every person at one time or another is confronted with disappointment and heartache; it is part of the price of being human that each of us must face despair—of varying degrees. Yet most of us would like to think that few people would choose to take their own lives as an escape from disaster. However, a growing number, particularly of young people, are taking this way out.

Sometimes, instead of destroying himself physically, a desperate man may commit social or spiritual suicide by withdrawing completely from his society or his God. Panicked by people or events, a man will try to back away, back down, or back out, to avoid a distasteful confrontation. And whenever a human being withdraws from the human race rather than face reality, the danger signal begins to flash.

For eventually the moment comes when an event or a person or a group of people will bring us face to face with ourselves or with whatever it is that we have been so carefully avoiding. And it is at this point that we, feeling suddenly trapped, become enraged at the person or circumstance that has forced our hand. So we lash out in our frustration and anger, bent on destroying the person who has threatened our ostrich security; for people, like hamsters, when they are caged in by their doubts or their own sense of inadequacy, eat each other up!

THE JUNGLE WITHIN

The jungle may be a far cry from the hamster cage, but the laws which operate in one are operative in the other.

There are many analogies being made today comparing man's condition with life on its most primitive level. The phrase, "the blackboard jungle," has been used by educators and columnists to describe the chaotic conditions in some of the nation's schools. People trying to work their way through metropolitan traffic have likened that maze to a jungle. The beat of the jungle is heard in much of today's music, and the law of the jungle pervades much of today's morality. Perhaps the jungle, in all reality, is not very far from any one of us, with jungle creatures prowling in the dark recesses of the human mind or crouching in the human heart. Adam and Eve may have been snared by a snake in the dim dawn of history; but man today is just as apt to fall prey to the python that winds itself silently around his inner being. The jungle may indeed be growing in the midst of us.

Dangerously hidden, cunningly coiled in the human heart, is man's own private python ready to squeeze out any person or idea that happens to threaten his prestige or position. It is this propensity for squeezing out life that is so terrifying, particularly when we realize that the children in some families frequently become the victims of the python complex of the parents. Let's see what happens when the python begins to wrap itself around a person.

A family had gone to a restaurant for supper, and they were giving the waitress their orders. Young Timmy said he wanted a hamburger.

"No," objected his mother. "You have

to order something besides a hamburger." Then, turning to the waitress, she said sternly, "He'll take the roast pork and dressing."

"But I don't want that! I'm not hungry enough for a big meal," pleaded the little boy. "I want a hamburger."

"You'll have what *I* say, and that's all there is to it," commanded the mother.

The waitress continued around the table. Then, as she turned to go out to the kitchen, she asked Timmy, "Do you want ketchup or mustard on your hamburger?"

"Ketchup!" he grinned. Then looking excitedly around the table he exclaimed, "She thinks I'm real!"

What a temptation it is for the adult to make the child conform. A certain amount of conformity is necessary, and many important disciplines are learned through the process of conforming. But conformity as an end in itself, or as a constant and unrelenting pressure, can be devastating to a child's growth; and yet, how unthinkingly a parent may bring out the python to perform the task of squeezing and shaping!

If the python sends a shudder through us, so also should the panther that pounces unexpectedly from some mysterious place within us. Again and again we find ourselves capitulating to what we might call the "panther psychosis," as we relegate our relationships to the law of the jungle.

We see the panther at work most clearly in the area of one of our most common paradoxes. We note that for some strange reason man, who in theory is supposed to desire life's best for his fellowman, in reality finds it easier to share grief and tragedy with others than to rejoice with them. Perhaps this is because when we feel sorry for someone, we somehow feel superior to him. And we like him, for *his* lack augments our own sense of security or our self-esteem. Lending a hand when a man is down requires relatively little of us, for we are gaining so much more than we are giving under these circumstances. And we can forgive a man a great deal when he is down and we are up! Giving solace to the sorrowing, alms to the beggar, and advice to the man in a quandary—these tokens of beneficence we give gladly.

By contrast, how grudgingly we give our "bravo" to the man who has surpassed us. We can scarcely bear to be outdone. So, to restore our sense of importance we turn our panther loose. We seize any little excuse to minimize another man's achievement, particularly if he has been in the same field of competition as ourselves. We search for a crack in his armor; and if we can find nothing to attack, we use the indirect method of innuendo. And because we are limited in our imaginations, we little guess what havoc may result when we turn the panther loose. And so the jungle

presses in on us

from every side.

But the thickest part of the jungle lies within us. There, if we look more closely, we find still another creature. This one is a bird of a different feather, in every sense of the word; and it has not been suspect, because it is so beautiful. What harm could possibly be hiding in the peacock's brilliant plumage?

Pride is the peacock parading in the human heart; and it is ironic that when others are most aware of our pride, we are least conscious of it.

The old saw, "Pride goeth before a fall," is one of the truest axioms ever uttered. Pride, as it is used in this quotation, does not refer to the variety which prompts courage and integrity. This type, which becomes a creative force in people's lives, used to be described in the early primers as "rightful pride," and this is something quite different from the destructive type of pride that is confining and self-centered. This negative form usually stems from a narrow desire to receive credit for something that has been accomplished. It has been aptly said that a lot more would get done in this world if we didn't care who got the credit.

One of the most poignant stories of the Old Testament revolves around the tender scene between David and his son Solomon. The king, once great but now advanced in years and acutely aware of his shortcomings, charges Solomon to build a temple for God. "My son, I had it in my heart to build a house to the name of the Lord my God" (I Chron. 22:7). Sorrowfully David has come to the realization that he cannot build the temple himself, because his life has fallen so short of God's commandments and his expectations of him. And so, just before the end, he puts aside his pride (and he has a lot of it to push away); then, relinquishing the honor he has coveted for so long, David gives Solomon the privilege of building the temple.

A proud strutter, King David had been the royal peacock of Israel. Over the years he had made a show of his wealth; he had used his power for selfish ends; and he had given in to the lusts and temptations of the times. To be sure, David the King had had some tall moments in his life, times when he had been the man of the hour. But he stood his tallest when, in complete humility, he was able to face up to the aggregate smallness of his life and admit that he wasn't the man for the job. At the end of his life he was able to conquer the peacock, his most dangerous foe. Hoping desperately that his son would be able to avoid the pitfalls he himself had known, David gave Solomon his fatherly advice and blessing: "May the Lord grant you discretion and understanding, that when he gives you charge over Israel you may keep the law of the Lord your God" (I Chron. 22:12). Our hearts go out to David—for we know, as he knew, the pressure of the jungle within.

One Christmas season, as I thought about the animals gathered around the manger, I wondered if there had once been a time when the sheep and the oxen had not been tame. Surely they had not always been so docile. Why, then, could not the beasts of the jungle be tamed as well? Figurative as the panther and the python were in the jungle of the human heart, they were, nevertheless, as devastating as if they had been real. Suddenly it occurred to me that the only escape from the jungle was to lay it out before the manger; and so I wrote my "Petition at Christmas":

So gently did they gather round
  The manger stall that night;
The sheep and cattle seemed to kneel
  Before thy Holy Light.

It was a night when everything
  Was reverently still;
All restless things, both man and beast,
  Bowed to thy Holy Will.

O thou, whose kindly gaze transformed
  The donkey's stubborn mind,
Lift me from out my python will
  That coils to choke and bind.

And thou, whose sure and steady voice
  Subdued the sheep's loud bleating,
Tame thou my panther, crouched to claw
  All whom I find competing.

Yes, thou whose gentle touch could calm
  The cattle's anxious lowing,
Touch thou the peacock in my soul,
  And keep my pride from growing.

O take the jungle from my heart
  And place thy manger there;
Shine thou thy star upon my life
  Until I learn to care.

THE HOURS THAT SHINE

I have frequently wondered why some manufacturer of games didn't develop one called "grope," in keeping with the general mood of the times. Playing a game like this, a person might just stumble upon some solutions to his problems as he worked his way around the board—from grope—to mope—to cope—and finally to hope (with a variety of other "ope" words in between).

But playing games has never really solved

people's problems; there has to be, instead, some kind of workable formula through which people can correct or improve their patterns of thought and action. One such happy and workable suggestion has come from the life of Harriet Beecher Stowe who, when the bottom dropped out of her world, was able to rebuild her life on the basis of an inscription on a sundial: *I count only the hours that shine.* These words soon became the moving force in Harriet's young life, pulling her to the very heights.

"The hours that shine" may sound to some like an untenable Pollyanna view of life. But if we examine the words more closely, we see that there is a significant difference between sunlit hours and the hours that shine. Oftentimes we discover that the hours that shine the brightest are not our carefree, sunlit hours at all; rather, they are the ones that have found us climbing out of the most dismal defeat, the bitterest hatred, the most crushing setback, or the most paralyzing illness. Time and again the most shining hours we know are the ones we have carved out of almost total loss or total failure.

If we have tested this by experience and believe it, then we have an obligation to help others see that the shining hours are not fashioned of sunlight alone; rather, they need the bas-relief of shadows to make them stand out and shine.

The humorist has taken the same basic philosophy of the sundial and has given it a slightly different fillip in his definition of the difference between an optimist and a pessimist. The difference, he observes, is this: the optimist says, "Good morning, God," while the pessimist says, "Good God—morning!"

There is a raucous chorus of critics who will immediately object to the apparent naïveté of "Good morning, God." "How theologically unsophisticated," they will say, compelled as they seem to be to reject the idea that man could possibly have a partner relationship with God. For the cynical sophisticate the concept of a partnership with the divine implies a selfish approach to the Almighty. Again and again the objection is raised: God is not a dispenser of band-aids; he is not a jovial genie, waiting for man's beck and call to wave away the hurt of a cut finger or a bleeding heart. And, to be sure, we can concur that if one's idea of partnership revolves around the saccharine Santa Claus approach, then certainly it is unacceptable.

But all too often, any hint of a personal

relationship with the Almighty or with his Son is so belittled that the seeking Christian is made to feel guilty for being so presumptuous as to claim any sort of kinship with the divine. The charge is often leveled that a person-to-person relationship with God is synonymous with intellectual shallowness or trivial belief. But it would seem to me that such a criticism does little except undermine the central message of the gospel.

If we deny the reality of the I-Thou relationship, what do we do with the heart of the New Testament? And would not the pulse of the Old Testament falter? Every significant relationship in the biblical narrative is a very personal one, whether it is the vertical God-man relationship or the horizontal man-man relationship. But any relationship will go awry if it becomes merely tangential; that is to say, if there is only a slight connection with God or with Christ or with our fellowman, then it is easy to grow detached and disinterested and eventually to become divorced from both divinity and humanity.

Some years ago, in one of my husband's former parishes, I spent the better part of an afternoon with a woman who was in the final days of a terminal illness. In the course of our conversation she made some observations which I have never forgotten, and the thread of her thoughts ran like this: "How I wish I could have my health back for just thirty days! How differently I would spend my time—I'd spend it with people. You know, there are all kinds of people I've been thinking about these past several weeks while I've been in bed—people whom I scarcely know, but whose friendship I'm sure I would have enjoyed. But now I'll never know them or be able to help them, because most of my time was always taken up with washing and dusting and cooking and ironing—and all the daily round of keeping house."

"But those things were important, too," I tried to assure her.

"Not *that* important," she replied, her eyes brimming with tears. "The routine jobs have taken up *all* my time." Then, after a slight pause, she continued wistfully, "You see, June, the dust always comes back, but the hours never do!"

In that sickroom, years ago, I felt suddenly overwhelmed by the tragedy of a woman who was realizing too late that though her pots and pans had always shone, she could count few, if any, shining hours. The emptiness that came from the lack of meaningful relationships made the physical illness even more desolate to bear.

Not always, but often, our personal interest in people seems to be in rather direct proportion to our personal awareness of the divine. If we think of God as a remote being, then it is not very difficult to keep people at a distance (perhaps what we may subconsciously be thinking of as a "safe distance"). How we view our relationship to God and how vital we make our relationship to Christ will have a definitive bearing on the type of relationship we have with people. And if we are to stop groping and begin coping and hoping again, we might find it wise to inscribe on our hearts the key words, "the hours that shine"!

PUTTING THE BEE ON

The twentieth century has many distinguishing characteristics, but few of them pose as intriguing a study as that provided by the mass mind.

Modern man is easily swayed, perhaps because he is bombarded with such a multitude of voices. And because the voices are so strident and there are so many of them, man feels a certain sense of security, however false, in following the loudest voice or

the one that is heard most often. Clustered around his creeds, flustered by his needs, man is vulnerable to the psychology of the mass.

The human situation reminds me of a rather unusual but significant truth that I learned one summer day from a swarm of bees.

Honeybees had buzzed into a walnut tree in our back yard and had formed a swarm heavy enough to make the branch sag several inches. The children were afraid to play in the yard when they saw the ominous cluster, and it soon became evident that something needed to be done.

Convinced that the safest solution to the problem was to call a friend who was a beekeeper, I asked him if he could help us get rid of the backyard menace. He came over in short order and asked if I had a good-sized cardboard carton and a garden hose.

"What on earth are you going to do with the hose?" I inquired in surprise.

"Watch!" he said.

He turned a fine spray of water on the swarm, soaking it thoroughly. Then, as I watched in utter amazement, he set the cardboard carton directly below the clump of bees and with one firm shake of the tree limb deposited the entire mass of bees inside the box. Calmly he closed the top of the carton and flashed a triumphant smile my way.

I must have looked completely nonplussed, for he proceeded with a succinct explanation of his successful strategy.

"You see," he said, "by turning the water on the swarm, I so thoroughly drenched the bees in the outer layer that they couldn't fly. And because they were immobile, they held in the rest of the swarm. And now I have the whole lot of them!"

I expressed my appreciation as well as my admiration for his expert handling of the matter.

"No trouble," he assured me, "no trouble at all."

The encounter with the bees keeps buzzing in my consciousness, and I cannot help noticing how like the swarm is our own human society. We allow a thin layer of people to imprison the rest. There is the "lunatic fringe" who may be "all wet," but their soggy morality or their shabby politics serve to dampen the efforts of the larger group; and, saddest of all, the larger group who would choose to have things different from the way they are, are rendered helpless by the pressures surrounding them.

In the life of the church we are too often

made ineffective by the wet blanket of the skeptic or the dash of cold water thrown by those who refuse to change, whose church is built not so much on the Rock of Ages as on the Middle Ages.

No doubt ever since the first drama was enacted on the stage of time, there have always been those who have opposed change. For these people, change—any kind of change—connotes a cataclysmic upheaval, and so they oppose it. And one does not debate with a brick wall.

At the opposite extreme are the people who have an insatiable desire for change. These are the ones who seldom, if ever, assess the merits of a particular change; they are the ones who are always clamoring about change for the sake of change!

Caught somewhere between the two extremes is the large majority of the populace who can readily understand the principle of playing both ends against the middle, for they are the middle.

A possible way out of the dilemma may be suggested by the following conversation which took place between a little girl and her mother. As the mother leaned over to kiss her young daughter good-night, the little girl said contentedly, "Mother, I've had such a happy time today!"

"Have you, my darling? And what made today different from yesterday?"

"Because," said the child, after a moment of reflection, "yesterday my thoughts pushed me around and today I pushed my thoughts around!"

A lot depends on who is doing the pushing. And the individual, though he may be part of the mass, must assert himself in order to keep the fresh breeze of reason blowing through his mind. The air tends to get rather stale in a huddled mass.

Concerned as we seem to be about finding ways out of our predicament, it is a pity that we try everything else first before coming to the door which has been standing open all the time: "If you continue in my word, you are truly my disciples, and you will know the truth, and the truth will make you free" (John 8:31-32).

The truth is, indeed, the key that will unlock us from within ourselves and free us from the tyranny of the mass. But we cannot ignore the first part of Christ's promise, for he did make a stipulation: "if you continue in my word."

How often we hear the quotation about the truth making us free! It has a noble ring and we like it, but we need to be mindful that the well-known second half of the quotation is incomplete without the lesser-known first half. Could it be that we have conveniently chosen to forget the opening words? Yet, without them, we may find ourselves as inextricably boxed in as the swarm of bees.

THREE HUNDREDTHS OF AN INCH

Modern man is caught in a wasteland of numbers. He is hemmed in by digits: on his tax form, his driver's license, his credit cards, his social security check, his zip code, his phone listing. And in all this proliferation of numbers we have all but lost sight of the meaning of "person." Sometimes it might even seem that God is little more than a serial number and heaven just another zip code.

In an age when the accent is on the assembly line, it seems more imperative than ever that we reread and recapture the excitement of many of the great Old Testament stories which put the emphasis on the individual. Reading these remarkable biographies, we cannot help but feel a new surge of pride in our humanity and a fresh awareness of the possibilities of the divine within each person.

In the vivid account of the siege of Jabesh-gilead, for example, as it is recorded in I Samuel, we are deeply stirred by the resolute stand taken by Saul—one lone individual who, motivated by courage and compassion, enlisted the help of a large force of men, who were then able to take action to save the people of Jabesh-gilead. One man by himself could not have made much difference. But one man, touched by God and helped by other men, turned the course of history.

The twentieth century has become so accustomed to underrating the individual and magnifying the mass that there has been a blurring of the belief that one person, one effort, one event can, indeed, make a difference and that the difference—if it is centered in God—can be very great.

From what we read we learn. But this

knowledge that we gain through books is augmented and enhanced by what we observe for ourselves. From the daily round of our common tasks we stumble upon still other pathways to truth. From each new venture comes some new vision.

Four years ago my son volunteered for the job of official weather observer for our area. The installation of the equipment and the instructions which accompanied the instruments opened up a new world of information for the whole family. We were introduced to a wide variety of facts, but perhaps the most surprising thing we learned was that volunteer weather observers are paid only if it rains (and then the rainfall must measure a minimum of half an inch within a twenty-four-hour period). This rather unusual criterion for remuneration was the source of considerable dismay for my son, who had had in mind something a little more substantial in the way of pocket money. However, being reasonably optimistic by nature, he took hope in the possibility that there might be enough summer thundershowers to make the weather station a fairly lucrative venture after all.

But, alas, that particular summer was unusually dry. There was no measurable rainfall for weeks; and the brighter the day, the gloomier my son's financial prospects! But then, one wonderful August afternoon, it rained. It rained hard! Excitedly we thought it had rained a couple of inches, and half an inch was all we needed for striking "pay dirt." Eagerly we lowered the measuring stick into the cylinder—but, alas, it had rained only forty-seven hundredths of an inch!

Sending a pleading look skyward, my son scanned the horizon for a cloud, one little cloud, that might be holding three hundredths of an inch more of rain. But there wasn't even the remnant of a cloud. Dejectedly emptying the rain gage, he sighed, "Well, we'll have to wait all over again."

What a difference three hundredths of an inch would have made that day! What a happy change there would have been in the outlook of one young boy if it had rained just that little bit more!

But therein lies the drama—and frequently the tragedy—of life. For too often the difference depends on as small a measure as that. We work and work at something for so long, and we tire of the effort. So we stop, never knowing that we came within three hundredths of an inch of achieving our goal. Or we give and give and give, and we grow so tired of giving that finally we stop, never guessing that one more gift, three hundredths of an inch, would have changed the course of a person's life, perhaps our own!

History is, in a sense, a record of measurements. Battles have been won—and lost—by three hundredths of an inch. People have been doomed—and redeemed—by such a small fraction as that! Love and hate, success and failure, have hung in the balance by three hundredths of an inch. Even the unfolding drama of the Christian faith can be told in fractions, for again and again God's kingdom has grown by three hundredths of an inch; and the New Testament abounds with examples.

But because we have become a people enamored with bigness, we seem to have little use in our day and age for bits and pieces. But the bits and pieces of our lives can be fitted together to make a significant pattern—if we are willing to forget our aversion to fractions. Each individual is, after all, only a fraction of the whole of humanity; nevertheless, we need to remember that it is quite possible for one life, even our own, to be the three hundredths of an inch that could make a special difference in God's total equation.

Truly, God has set Jabesh-gilead in the midst of us; and if we are to claim it, we can count no effort too small.

STRUCTURED OR STRICTURED?

In our multifaceted culture we hear a good deal about structures and structuring. Even the novice can sound reasonably astute as he sprinkles his conversation with the phraseology of the high-rise apartment and the split-level marvels of steel and glass.

The church has borrowed the current idiom and is also busily structuring and re-structuring. And so, as this trend has been felt and expressed in our religious and secular life alike, it may be that the 1960's will be remembered someday as the Decade of the Structure.

But is it possible that our obsession with structure may so stricture our thoughts that we will be able to think only in terms of rigid, predetermined forms?

The two words, "structure" and "stricture," are somewhat deceptive. They are look-alikes, but they are quite different in meaning. However, like two railroad tracks that seem to converge when seen from a distance, these two words reach a point at which they may also appear to merge.

There is but a single letter that separates "structure" from "stricture"; but their meanings provide a wider separation. A structure is a building or construction, in a literal or figurative sense; a stricture is a binding or constriction—again, in a literal or figurative manner of speaking.

Occasionally, as has already been pointed out, a structure may become a stricture. For example, in a Sunday school class when a definition of "church" is requested, somebody will invariably say, "The church is a building." In this case, then, a building may indeed become a binding as it holds the mind to a narrow view of what the church is.

Unfortunately some people never do graduate from this level of thinking about the church; and, as a natural result, their churchmanship is very limited. Structures are necessary, certainly, for a well-ordered life and for effective performance; but if a particular structure (whether a building or a system of thought) becomes the be-all and the end-all of existence, then the structure deteriorates to being merely a stricture.

I have a friend who is ninety-five years old, active, witty, and keenly interested in people and events. His life holds ample evidence of the rewards of creative structuring. From his earliest years he has developed the ability to establish an orderly sequence of days, based on a simple but meaningful value structure. Every morning he keeps office hours and holds himself to the discipline of doing what needs to be accomplished before noon. Then, because he has worked toward a specific goal each morning, he is free the remainder of the day to enjoy his friends, his thoughts, his outings, and his dreams.

Just before his ninety-fifth birthday he was to be honored by the high school student body as the community's outstanding senior citizen. He was deeply touched by this honor, and he looked forward with happy anticipation to the day on which the special recognition assembly was to be held. But when the day arrived, he was confined to his bed with a severe cold. Disappointed at not being able to go, but undaunted by fever and chills, he spent the better part of the morning writing an essay which could then be read to the students when the award was made to him *in absentia* that afternoon.

He wrote about the school he had attended when he was a boy in a little prairie town struggling for existence and identity. He set down a simple but vivid description of the classroom, with its spartan surroundings. But there was such an undertone of respect and affection in the essay that it mitigated the mood of austerity which surrounded those early years. With characteristic humor he wrote, "There was no inside plumbing (this produced problems not entirely academic!)."

Toward the end of his delightful essay, the nonagenarian made this significant observation as he arrived at the heart of the matter: "In those days the idea of going to school and studying—in fact the very important reason for studying—was to get an education and not to be entertained."

This man, throughout the experiences of

a ninety-five-year span, had learned to put first things first. And he had been able to do this because, at an early age, he had apparently acquired the important art of sifting.

Sifting is basic to structuring; the separating of the chaff from the wheat must be the prelude to any sort of enduring performance. But to be able to translate this idea into the motions of the daily round demands a rugged discipline. It is pleasanter to rationalize that one's days should be flexible and one's duties kept fluid.

In the work of the church, for instance, very likely the reason a lot of important jobs never get done is that too many people, like myself, prefer to do the convenient thing, or the enjoyable thing, rather than the necessary thing. Like my own faltering witness, others are also neglecting to structure their activities on the basis of priorities, with the result that their witness is also weakened. How much less strictured one's conscience would be if one could learn to do the important job first, then the next most important, and the next and the next —as strength and time allowed.

When Christ said, "Seek first," these were no idle words he was using. He was anxious to assure us that no matter whether we are on the giving end or the receiving end, the secret of fulfillment lies in the simple statement of priorities: "Seek first his kingdom and his righteousness, and all these things shall be yours as well" (Matt. 6:33).

PROCRASTINATION PUSHES THE PANIC BUTTON

Procrastination must surely rank close to the top of the list of common human frailties. It is a plague to young and old alike, and it is not limited to any geographic grouping. How far-reaching it is became very clear to me in a conversation which my husband had one evening with a Finnish exchange student who was living in our home.

"Have you done all your homework?" my husband asked.

"Ahhyyeeeeesssss," replied the boy.

It hadn't taken us long to learn that "ahhyyeeeeesssss" in that particular tone of voice meant that he *hadn't* finished his homework. So my husband prodded him a little more. "We have a good maxim in English, you know, that says you should never put off till tomorrow what you can do today."

"Oh, but to say it the other way around is also very good," countered our student. "Never do today what you can put off till tomorrow!"

"But," argued my husband, "you might not even *be* here tomorrow!"

"Aah, that is *why* you shouldn't do today . . . !"

Delightfully disarming as the young man's wit was, his outlook left something to be desired.

Many times since then I have thought how typical it is of a great many of us to postpone the unpleasant, to hide around the corner from the inevitable encounter, or to sidestep the decision that has to be made. But then comes the moment when someone or something makes us focus our attention on the very thing we have tried to ignore. And when this happens, how painful the moment of reckoning is! But we have to face it.

I recall all too vividly one of those apocalyptic moments, which arrived for me one spring morning after a prolonged period of procrastination. I had gone to a friend's home to meet with an ecumenical Bible study group, and we had just begun our discussion when the telephone rang. The hostess answered it, then beckoned to me. It was my husband calling to let me know that a parsonage building committee from a neighboring town had just phoned to say they would be arriving in twenty minutes to have a tour of our relatively new parsonage.

As I replaced the receiver I sank in a sea of mixed emotions. I was deeply grateful to my husband for calling to alert me; I was righteously indignant (inadequate phrase) at the committee that was coming on such short notice; and I was panic-stricken by my contemplation of the condition of the house.

Excusing myself hastily from the study group, I hurried home to see if there was any way of salvaging a bad situation. The past few days had been unusually hectic, with the result that my efforts at housekeeping had deteriorated to a bare minimum. En route home I remembered how grateful I had been for an excuse to go out somewhere that morning, because the house had so closely resembled a major disaster area.

The breakfast dishes had been left on the kitchen counter, because the sink was filled with the supper dishes from the night before. None of the beds had been made yet. The furniture had had a vacation from the dustcloth for several days. In fact, the only housework I had done that morning before leaving the house was the sorting of the laundry, which now was lying in four dismal piles on the utility room floor.

I walked into the back hallway and immediately wished there were some means of escape. But escape lay only in myself.

Then, quite unexpectedly, like a flash of lightning coming from the melee of thoughts tumbling around in my head, there blazed a phrase that I had read long ago in an English class: "Do ye nexte thynge!" It was an old inscription that dated back to the period of Donne or Chaucer. I couldn't recall any of the background of the epigram; no doubt it was the great-great-grandmother of all the household hints that have since been penned. The sentence stood out sharply in my memory, as if I had just learned it for a test, and it was sufficient for my need.

"Do ye nexte thynge"—so I did it, after taking a quick survey and making a mental list of priorities. I did the most urgent thing first. Fortunately I have a large oven; so when all the dirty dishes were cached in that, I tackled the biggest bedroom, hoping that if I still had some time left I could go on to straighten up the next bedroom and the next.

Fortunately for me, and for them, the committee was a little late in getting to the house. It was surprising how much I was able to accomplish in those extra fifteen minutes.

The experience had been a frantic one, but it taught me a most valuable lesson. I realized that I had fallen into the habit of directing my efforts and energies toward the smaller jobs first, leaving the larger tasks until last. When I began to regain my equilibrium, following my housecleaning blitz, it occurred to me that if I had fallen into such a slipshod pattern in my housekeeping duties, perhaps there were other areas of my life that needed examination and revision.

Procrastination pushed my panic button and rang a bell that I needed to hear!

THE SEARCH FOR SOLVENCY

With the fragmentation of family life and the current hue and cry about the generation gap, we might well consider the need for strengthening the homes of our nation; for a nation is only as strong as the individual families which comprise its citizenry. But whenever we set about strengthening something, we must first try to discover where the weaknesses are so that our efforts at improvement may be as meaningful as possible.

The awareness of one of the basic weaknesses at the core of our culture came to me in the course of my duties as a judge at a speech contest which was being held for senior high members of a particular organization. In the division of extemporaneous speaking, to which I had been assigned, there was a choice of four topics from which each contestant could select one. A half hour was allowed for preparation of the speech, five minutes in which to deliver it, and a final minute or two in which to clarify any points about which the judges might raise questions.

Although the contestants had come from twelve or thirteen counties, it was interesting to note that five of the eight boys in my division happened to choose the same topic—one which dealt with the role of their organization in providing leadership for the future. I was eager to see how these boys would develop their theme, but I was disappointed that in the course of their talks none of the five boys really defined "leadership." And yet, in spite of the lack of a definition, I couldn't help noticing that each boy conveyed the strong implication that leadership had a lot to do with financial success.

During the question period I asked the boys to explain a little more specifically what they meant by "leadership." They all expressed the idea that a good leader was someone who had made a success of his occupation or profession, someone who had been able to "get ahead in the world," someone who had reached "the top" (regardless of what methods might have been used to achieve the top). Implicit in all the answers was the underlying conviction that financial solvency and success were prime requisites for attaining positions of leadership.

This emphasis on financial solvency became so troublesome to me as the day wore on that the first thing I did after arriving home was to see what the dictionary had to say about "solvency." It was a provocative definition: "Solvency is the ability to meet all claims."

The speech contestants, in putting all the emphasis on financial solvency, were ignoring two other areas of solvency which were equally, if not more, important. Now, having mulled over these thoughts for some time, I cannot help feeling that if it is important to be able to meet our financial claims, it is just as vital for us to be able to meet the intellectual and spiritual claims that are made upon us from day to day. But then the question arises as to whose responsibility it is to foster the solvency of the mind and the solvency of the spirit. The triumvirate of home and church and shcool *should* be able to nurture this inner solvency, but for some reason the job isn't getting done.

How might we, then, rediscover the steps which lead to the solvency of the mind and the spirit so that we and our children may, indeed, be able to meet all claims? We most assuredly cannot give to our children anything we do not have ourselves. And, whether we like it or not, our children may be rather close to the truth when they say that adults are triangles—and according to their definition, a triangle is a square with something missing.

We might not have to look too far to find that what is missing is the reassuring awareness of consistency which our children need to see in our pronouncements and our actions. Inconsistency can sever a relationship about as quickly as any other fault; it crumbles confidence and creates a credibility gap that becomes almost impossible to bridge.

Perhaps we might cite two or three examples of the kind of inconsistency that our children must surely find dismaying. For example, at the same time that we adults are demanding high academic achievement from our children, we ourselves are satisfied with lapsing into an intellectual fog, reading whatever requires the least effort and parroting the predigested ideas that feed our pet prejudices. Or we will reprimand our children for arriving late at the dinner table, while we ourselves are chronically late when going to pick them up after school. Then, again, we will admonish our children sternly about cheating in an examination while, on the other hand, we will stretch a point to evade a penalty or do some fancy doubletalk to dodge something difficult.

If we are to encourage the search for solvency, we must first admit that such solvency begins with intellectual honesty and has to be nurtured by a spiritual integrity that refuses to be compromised. And only as our children come to sense the inner consistency at the power center of our lives will they be able to achieve a solvency of their own that is not based solely on the checkbook balance.

FRESH BREEZE BLOWING

Trite and timeworn as the old adage may be that "necessity is the mother of invention," it is still based on a valid rationale. The principle can be applied equally well to the imaginative use of material things as to the resourceful arrangement of intangibles. And it is always exhilarating to discover in the dormant present an "open sesame" to some new and unsuspected future joy. Fortunate it is that now and then we do stumble upon a situation that helps us rediscover some muscle we'd forgotten we had. We may groan a bit at the sudden exertion, but the feeling of aliveness always seems to more than make up for the temporary discomfort.

This was my experience in an encounter which turned out much more happily than I had imagined possible at the outset. I had been asked to pinch-hit for a speaker who had become ill the day before a special club program on modern art. "But," I protested, when asked to fill in, "I don't know anything about modern art; and, what's more, I don't even like it!"

"Well, you'll just have to like it for one night," said the program chairman soothingly as she left me with less than eighteen hours to get an art lesson together.

I didn't sleep a bit well that night, tossing and turning in anticipation of the tall order I had to fill on the morrow. I was downtown early the next morning; and after finding a few volumes on modern art, I began to do some frantic skipreading. The more I read, the less I knew. Finally, however, I came across what seemed to be a key idea. The modern artist does not draw what he sees, I learned; he draws, instead, what he feels. This statement gave me an idea, which I promptly tried out.

When my unsuspecting husband came home for lunch, I placed two blank sheets of paper and a box of crayons in front of him. Then I asked him to draw whatever he might feel while listening to two very different kinds of mood music which I played for him. The experiment with the records and the crayons proved to be sufficiently stimulating and entertaining to warrant my doing the same type of thing that evening as part of my presentation at the club meeting.

When I announced that we were going to do some drawing, the club women were aghast. "Heavens!" exclaimed one horrified member. "I haven't drawn anything since the sixth grade!" But when I assured the group that what they drew didn't really have to resemble anything just so long as it expressed what they felt, the ladies relaxed and let their creativity go to work. By the end of the evening they had produced some highly expressive compositions in color and design.

The evening touched some long-silent chords for many of the women. And for me it brought the exciting realization that I had been made to stretch my own mind to a new dimension, to study something about which I had been skeptical, to be jostled out of my comfortable mental ruts.

Since that time I have done a fair amount of additional reading in the controversial but stimulating area of modern art; and I can even see some merit now in the baffling painting entitled "Eggbeater Number 3"!

The whole experience had been like a sailboat ride with the tingling exuberance of heading into a bracing wind. But how close I had come to missing the boat altogether! And I thought fleetingly of the many other boats I probably *had* missed over the years, and I felt a strange and wistful longing within me.

When one has made a voyage, one must always make another. For when the mind has puffed its sails and has felt the joy of leaning into the wind, it can never again be entirely content to lie at anchor in the safe haven of the familiar and the ordinary.

CANDLES IN THE HAMBURGERS

It was my older daughter's seventeenth birthday, and I had looked forward to a leisurely enjoyment of this special occasion. But the day had become bogged down with interruptions. Suddenly it was suppertime, and the birthday cake still hadn't been baked. And the kind of supper I had planned to prepare just hadn't materialized. So we sat down to hamburgers. They had been dressed up a little with the family's favorite sauce, but still—they were hamburgers.

As we drew our chairs up to the table, I felt more keenly than ever the need for some sort of birthday symbol, however small it might be. So I hurried to the cupboard, took out the package of birthday candles, and put one in the center of each meat patty.

The sheer absurdity of candles in the hamburgers had a magical effect. Immediately a party mood was established, and the hilarity mounted as we discovered that the heat of the hamburgers was melting the base of the candles. Despite the absence of the customary birthday trappings, the day had been redeemed.

After supper the children attended a concert with some of their friends. While they were gone, I scurried around to bake a cake so that when the group stopped back at the house I could invite everyone to stay for some light refreshments.

As the girls were chatting around the table, one of them turned to me and said with an appreciative grin, "What a great idea you had at supper!" I shot a look of mock reproof at my daughter. The happy twinkle in her eyes confirmed my suspicion that she had told the girls the whole ridiculous story. Then, as the merriment began to subside, one of the girls said with a wistful little sigh, "I wish our family was the kind that could have candles in the hamburgers."

Her words sent a surge of gratitude through me. How thankful I was that somehow I had stumbled upon something to enhance the commonplace that day. And how simple it had been!

There it was—simplicity, the guideline for any genuinely meaningful or redemptive act. But, caught up as we are in protocol and elaborate preparations for the things we do, we find it a struggle to simplify. If we could, though, how much more readily we might redeem a situation—or a person. But too much of the time, too many of us continue to cling to the mistaken notion that people are impressed with the complex and the ornate; whereas if the truth were known, we no doubt would find that most people are suspicious of the grandiose as being nothing more than empty show.

As we look at the invitations of Christ, we cannot help noticing their exceeding simplicity: come, come and see, follow, rise, watch, take heed, go, stretch out your hand, have no fear, feed my sheep.

The Way is set forth in the simplest of

terms, conveying a refreshing purity and sweetness. But we who have grown accustomed to the complex cloverleaf interchanges of our superhighways have come to think that any road, to be worthy of the name, should be an intricate marvel of engineering ingenuity. If it's complicated, it must be good: this is the questionable theorem on which we base so much of our thinking. We no longer want a simple, old-fashioned route to anything, whether we're traveling on vacation or planning a birthday celebration—or searching for a faith. We are sophisticated; at any rate we think we are, and we want all of life to be dressed up in psychedelic colors, even our religion. Consequently, person after person makes his pilgrimage to spiritual identity a complicated and frustrating quest. Who knows, perhaps the first step of our journey needs to be lighted by something as unlikely as candles in the hamburgers.

THE SOUND OF SLUSH

More and more, whether we are traveling via the nation's interstate system or by supersonic jet, our prime consideration seems to be to get there fast. Our impatience has seeped into every compartment of our lives, even the realm of the spirit. We want to see results; we want to get there in record time.

The only conditions that slow our pace seem to be fog and ice. And every driver and pilot knows how hair-raising it is to be obliged to make a trip when the roads are like glass or when visibility is nil.

I recall a drive I had to make one winter evening to a meeting that was about seventy miles from my home. The highway was coated with a treacherous layer of sleet, and my heart was in my mouth as I moved my car along at a cautious twenty-five miles an hour. The first thirty miles were a nightmare. But I kept going, pinning my hopes on the possibility that because my route lay south I might soon drive out of the band of ice.

All of a sudden I heard the sound I had been waiting for—the reassuring sound of slush under my wheels! There was traction for my car, and a great wave of relief engulfed me.

As I thought about this sudden and very welcome change in the condition of the highway, I felt that it held within it a parable of the condition of man's soul. We frequently discover that the soul, like the highway, is coated over; but the coating of the soul takes infinitely longer to break through—for there we find the glaze of greed or the sleet of shame or, worst of all, the hard ice of hate.

I thought back to a frightening experience I had had some months earlier when, in the course of trying to act as an intermediary in an unnecessary misunderstanding, I had uncovered a bitter and unyielding hatred. The encounter had been so devastating that I had brooded over it for many days. Then, feeling that I had to rid my mind of the ugliness I had seen, I poured out my anguish in a few brief lines of verse. What I wrote was certainly not good poetry, but the writing of the poem provided the catharsis that I needed:

Precariously we stood at anger's edge,
Where truth and friendship have so often died;
But, hoping love might lift us from this ledge,
I said, "Please listen to the other side."

"Perhaps there is another side, but I
Don't want to hear it," you replied;
Your lips were trembling, and I wondered why
You clung so to the precipice of pride.

I felt my hope, like crumbling earth, give way;
Your words had blocked the path
and torn the chart.
Quite suddenly the sky had turned to gray—
I heard the sound of shriveling
in my heart.

From this experience and from what I had discovered in driving my car that icy night, I found a formula that helped me clarify an area of my thinking that had for a long time remained fuzzy. It now seems evident to me that before anything significant can happen to change the human condition, there must be a melting, a breaking up of the treacherous coating on our lives. The Holy Spirit must be able to hear the reassuring sound of slush in a man's soul before any progress can be made. The melting takes so terribly long, sometimes; and yet the process involved is so simple.

Warmth acts on ice to change its form. Christ's love melts the frozen wasteland of a man's life and transforms it. It is as simple as that. So, instead of trying to complicate our circumstances, can we not graciously accept the gift of sun in our sky?

LET US GO TO GOULIMINE!

"Do you suppose there really is a place called Goulimine?" asked one of my daughters late one night.

"Goo-lee-meen?" I queried, copying her pronunciation. "How do you spell it?"

"G-o-u-l-i-m-i-n-e."

"I never heard of it, but I suppose there is such a place," I replied casually. "Why do you ask?"

"Well," she said dreamily, "I saw such

an unusual ad in a magazine a few days ago, and it said that Goulimine was fifty days by camel from Timbuktu. It made me sort of curious as to whether the place was real or imaginary."

"I'm sure it must be real," I replied, going on to explain. "Timbuktu is real, you know, even though we usually hear about it only in the expression, 'from here to Timbuktu'; so no doubt Goulimine is a real place too, even though it may sound too exotic and far away to be real."

"Let's find it!" suggested my daughter eagerly.

"At midnight?" I asked.

"It should only take a few minutes," she countered.

Our atlas, which would have simplified our search, had been loaned to a neighbor's child the day before; so we hunted up some old maps and began the quest. We were hampered further by the lack of two small but valuable bits of information. The ad hadn't stated whether Goulimine was north, east, south, or west of Timbuktu; nor had it mentioned how far a camel could travel in *one* day, let alone fifty.

We combed the deserts of North Africa; our index fingers traveled in every direction across the map. And finally, more than an hour later, we found Goulimine. We felt as triumphant as if we had struck oil.

Somehow it didn't matter that it was scandalously late for a school night, because my daughter and I had found more than Goulimine that night. We had found each other!

It had been a hectic spring, and our family's activities had begun to resemble the gyrations of a whirling dervish. I had had very little time to spend with any of the children, either together or individually. Instinctively my daughter and I both knew that we needed to find Goulimine, and that we needed to find it together. We had had nothing to go by, no chart or compass except the need in our hearts. But this was enough for making the journey.

At some point in every person's life he must find Goulimine. It is more than a place on the map; it is a need to be fulfilled—and it has many names.

In the biblical account of man's journey, there are many Goulimines:

> Arise, go to Nineveh!
> Come over to Macedonia!
> Get you up to a high mountain!
> And he set sail for Troas.
> He set his face toward Jerusalem.

Goulimine is wherever a man must go to find himself or to find his Lord or to fulfill his destiny. And in the course of a lifetime he may have to make the journey more than once. He may discover that Goulimine is in a different place every time he goes; for needs change as a man changes, and the Goulimine of his childhood may not satisfy him as a man.

Goulimine does have, nonetheless, a universal location. It is in the deep center of every man's heart. It is as near to him as breathing; yet it sometimes takes a very long time to get there.

Christ confronted those who wanted to follow him with the possibility of making a journey. He offered a destination; but because it sounded so foreign, they hesitated. It seemed safer to travel the familiar paths.

We are not much different today. The Goulimine of the spirit is too often thought of as a forbidden city, a mythical place we cannot possibly attain. Yet we do not seem to be reluctant to set out to find our financial Goulimine; nor do we hesitate to seek our Goulimine socially or intellectually. It is only the quest for our spiritual Goulimine that gives us pause.

For some strange reason it appears easier to sit still and enjoy the fruits of our labors rather than to sample the fruits of the spirit. Ironically, modern man—who is very much of a pioneer at heart—still hesitates to explore the most exciting frontier of all. And he does not quite comprehend that unless the journey is made, the sands of neglect may well drift over the once-marked trail—and Goulimine will lie crumbling in the heart of us all.

WAVELENGTHS

We are hearing much nowadays about communication. The word is used in many contexts: communication media, communication lag, breakdown in communications, failure to communicate.

Someone has facetiously said that we communicate best with those whose degree of confusion is the same as our own. Or, to take this idea out of the realm of the jest, we may say that we communicate most readily with people who are "on our wavelength."

There is something akin to an electrical charge that leaps from one mind to another when the people who are engaged in a conversation share a common excitement about the subject under discussion. However, it is not just the words by themselves which convey what we are saying. Equally important in the interplay between people are the facial tensions, the voice inflections, the gestures of the hands, and even the positions in which the people are sitting.

Volumes have been written about the art of speaking and the art of listening, but nothing much has ever been written about that nebulous sixth sense or seventh sense or whatever it may be that either establishes rapport or disrupts it. A person may have the finest diction in the world or the most erudite vocabulary and still not be able to communicate adequately with anyone. On the other hand, a person may not say a word and still communicate a great deal.

The intrinsic quality of a person comes through; and though we may not be able to define it, we recognize it at once. And there are other criteria, certainly, which play a part in our first impressions and help formulate our lasting impressions.

To "speak the same language," whether this phrase is taken literally or figuratively, is also worth working for, because new relationships keep opening up as we learn to communicate with a broader spectrum of our society.

Occasionally we are puzzled by the innovations in our language, particularly as we hear familiar words used in a new context. But if we listen carefully, it is usually possible to guess the new meanings.

For instance, one summer day when my son was talking on the phone to one of his friends, I noticed that he used the adjective "hairy" a number of times in describing something he was pleased about—at any rate I assumed these were things that pleased him, judging from the enthusiastic tone of his voice when he referred to having seen a "real hairy movie" or having heard a "hairy song" or having bought the "hairiest shirt." It seemed an odd adjective, but it was evident from his inflection that this was the latest "in" word for describing things that were especially enjoyed or admired.

I was thankful, a few days later, that I had already been introduced to this particular word and that I understood it; otherwise it might have been rather startling to hear my son observe, as I was leaving for a party,

"Gee, Mom, you look hairy!" He was paying me a high compliment—though this certainly wouldn't have been evident from the literal meaning of his words!

I have wondered if we are sometimes so literal that we fail to listen. Occasionally are we not all guilty of the kind of mind-set that Christ may have been referring to when he observed, "They have ears but they hear not"? How much we miss when we fail to tune our ears to the new sounds around us, however strange some of them may seem to be. But if we could stop complaining about not hearing very well, we might be surprised at how many of the new sounds would then come through on our particular wavelength. Perhaps by developing what we might call the stewardship of listening we could open up an exciting new frontier of human understanding.

DIMESTONES

The first thought that might occur to a person looking at the word "dimestones" is that there has been a typographical error. But such is not the case. It is, rather, a brand-new word, one coined by my younger daughter and one which gives a person's imagination considerable latitude.

The word was born on a winter afternoon while my two daughters were playing in the snow. They came into the house briefly to dry their mittens and warm their hands; and while they were sitting cuddled up to the radiator, the younger of the girls told me that she and her sister had built a snow palace. Then, with her brown eyes shining, she announced that her sister had let her be the queen. "And do you know what?" she concluded triumphantly, "I wore *dimestones!*"

It was a delightful blend of two words, "diamonds" and "rhinestones." And it conveyed a fascinating new idea to me. Dimestones was a perfect word for describing what happens when we try to combine the genuine with the false, which is something people seem to be very good at doing. Our human relationships with one another are full of dimestones: the compromises, the half-truths, the exaggerations, the scheming, the empty flatteries, the apple-polishing, and the vacillations. And until we can ferret out these inconsistencies in our attitudes and motives and in our whole range of relationships, we have no very sound base on which to construct either a creed or a lifework.

When I consider all the dimestones that we "average Christians" offer to God, I must confess there is reason to blush. We offer so little from out of our abundance;

and even the little that we do offer is more often silver plate than sterling—whether we're speaking of our material gifts or the gifts of service and devotion.

Sometimes I wonder if we might not have something to learn from men of other faiths, whose sense of gratitude and level of giving too often surpass ours. I recall that when I lived in Japan the servant in our home had a small ancestral shrine in her room, and every evening she brought an offering of food to the altar. She always took the first portion of the rice and the first sampling of the fish and laid these firstfruits at the entrance of her shrine.

I often think of O-ba-san and her devotion to her non-Christian faith when I note the reluctance of average Christians to bring *our* firstfruits to the altar of our God. This holding back is felt across the whole church, for we who call ourselves followers of the Way do not follow very well. Too much of the time we bring to our altar only what's left over; and God is lucky, sometimes, that there is anything at all! We wait to see how things are going to work out, and then we decide how much we can spare. Usually it's not much.

What a pity it is that this should be the case at a time when it is so vitally important for the Christian to be communicating the most dynamic witness possible; for, like vultures, the critics of the Christian faith hover over our lives, waiting to swoop down to pick at the dry bones of our apathy. And still, in spite of the urgency of the times, we continue along the path of the dimestone prayers, the dimestone effort, and the dimestone loyalty. And over and over we lay our dimestone gifts on his altar.

Is it any wonder, then, that those outside the Christian faith should ask us casually, "Were you saying something?"

BARTERING WITH GOD

If we run into as many complications communicating with God as we do in conveying meanings to our fellow human beings, then we might conclude that praying can become a rather precarious venture. However, it may be that the actual words we use trouble God far less than the attitudes we bring to our moments of communion with him.

I wonder what the Almighty must think

of our "barter approach," for instance. This is the technique we use when we promise him something in exchange for something we want from him. To set this down in black and white sounds crass indeed, for we probably had not thought of what we do as "bartering." But essentially this is what the process involves.

The first time I became aware of the barter system of prayer was during a siege of rough weather on a long plane trip. The jet I was on appeared to be riding on the coattails of a ferocious storm, and I became very apprehensive. Even under the most auspicious circumstances I am not overly fond of flying, so my state of agitation increased with every sharp downdraft and every sudden updraft we encountered. Doubtful that I would ever reach the ground in one piece, I turned instinctively to the Almighty and made a very rash promise. "O, God," I blurted out in a silent, desperate bargain, "if you'll just get me down on the ground safely, I promise I'll never get on a plane again!"

Even as I said the words I knew they were hypocritical. For in the light of tightly scheduled engagements and complicated travel connections, I was sure I would have to rely on planes often in making future plans. And yet, in spite of what I knew in my heart, I still made God an offer. I would sacrifice the convenience of air travel in exchange for his guarantee of a safe landing for the jet I was on.

Looking back on that experience, I wonder if the Almighty didn't chuckle a little to himself. Or maybe he heaved a heavy sigh at this further evidence of our human foibles and frailties.

Equally mystifying to God must be our strategy of flattery. This is never so evident as in some of the prayers one hears in services of formal worship. The moment comes for the pastoral prayer, for example; God is addressed, then he is described by such an impressive list of attributes that one might almost think that an after-dinner speaker was being introduced.

By contrast there is Mary's simple, direct acknowledgment of God's greatness: "My soul doth magnify the Lord."

And similar in tone is the simple eloquence of the Breton fisherman's prayer: "Dear God, be good to me; the sea is so big and my boat is so small."

Seldom are we humble enough to reduce ourselves to the essential core of our being. We like to be all dressed up—or puffed up. And all the time we go on hoping that God will be tolerant and benevolent and that we will not have to feel the sting of his displeasure.

Having gotten ourselves into such a dilemma, we search frantically for a way out of it. But there is no way out until we have first defined our problem. And in defining it we might find a helpful clue in a rather intriguing Greek word, *hamartia,* which means "sin," but which, when translated literally, means "to miss the mark." Now if we may take the liberty of creating an anglicized adjective from this old Greek word, in order to describe the general caliber of our Christian stewardship, we could say that a large share of the time we practice a "hamartian" stewardship. In other words, we rationalize that we are doing our part; but when we are entirely honest with ourselves, we have to admit that a lot of the time we are missing the mark. And we might as well admit that part of this business of missing the mark has something to do with our penchant for bartering with God. He does not condescendingly move our target to a more convenient angle so we can hit it every time.

WHERE THE WATER ISN'T

Little everyday dramas that take place in the playhouse of the family circle often become milestones in the dramas of our wider relationships. A word, a gesture, a picture —these suddenly bring to mind some half-forgotten event. So it was that the picture of a rustic bridge recalled for me a minor family drama that took place some years ago.

I had come home from town with groceries for supper. The children met me at the door in a flurry of excited animation. "Come see what we've got!" they exclaimed, pulling me into the bathroom. There, in the half-filled tub, swam three or four rather large bullheads.

I learned that one of our neighbors had gone fishing and had caught more than he could use, so he had brought some over to us.

"Do you know how to clean them?" I asked my son, who was about ten years old at the time.

"No," he admitted.

"Well, neither do I," I said. "And since Dad isn't going to be home until late tonight, probably we'd better take the fish back to the stream and turn them loose."

Reluctantly the children agreed that this was the best thing to do, so we put the fish in a bucket of water and drove out to the nearby stream. I parked as close as I could to the embankment. Since I couldn't pull the car completely off the road, I felt I should stay in the car in case I needed to move it. The children took the bucket of fish—but instead of clambering down the slope to the water to turn the bullheads loose, much to my astonishment they ran over to the middle of the bridge and emptied the bucket from there.

I hadn't expected them to put the fish back that way; so when the children returned to the car, I asked anxiously, "Did you aim the fish into the river all right?"

"Yes," they replied.

"But are you sure they got back in the water?" I asked.

"Yes, Mother," they chorused, trying to be tolerant of my continued questioning.

But I still wasn't completely satisfied as to the fate of the bullheads, so I asked another question or two.

Finally in utter exasperation one of the children blurted out, "Mother, do you think the bridge would have been built over where the water *wasn't?*"

How profound are the questions children ask!

I have thought of this particular query more than once; and by enlarging the idea implicit in the original question, I have found at least part of the reason for the shabby witness of our average Christianity.

Building bridges over where the water isn't—perhaps this is one of the factors that contribute to our wavering witness. We have done a fairly good job of convincing ourselves that we are meeting the needs of the world around us; but the fact of the matter is that much of our frenetic activity has little purpose. So we are merely busy being busy.

The church, individually or collectively, is occasionally tempted to circumvent an issue or to produce a solution that will be easier and more acceptable, instead of addressing itself to the specific need that is really there. Because we sometimes find ourselves in the embarrassing position either of having no answer for a given question, or not wanting to give the answer that we know is required of us, we try to change the question. "Just ask the right questions," we implore. "Ask only the questions for which we do have answers," we plead.

Christ never offered to fill needs that were theoretical rather than real. He didn't go about with a book of a hundred and one right answers tucked under his arm, hoping that people would ask the hundred and one right questions. No, he was the kind of person who always built his bridge where the water was, even if the torrent was swift and exceedingly dangerous.

Why is it that we who claim to be bridge builders in his name are so afraid of deep water, of fast-moving water? Why do we back away so quickly when we learn that building the bridge may demand our all? Why have we so few answers for the *wrong* questions? Why have we allowed ourselves to become the fellowship of the faint-hearted, the brotherhood of the back-off? As we search for answers to these questions, we must stop building our bridges over where the water isn't. Rather, we must build them for a purpose so that they will surely lead to the Way, the Truth, and the Life.

SPLIT-LEVEL AND MAROONED

In every community, in the gathered church or the scattered church, there is an urgent need for a ministry to the marooned, a ministry to those people whose lives have been cut off from the main current of activity. In our very midst there is a shockingly large number of people who live on islands: islands of loneliness or illness, islands of misunderstanding, islands of poverty, and islands that have no name but are still islands, nonetheless. By and large, efforts to reach these insular souls are only sporadic; consequently, most of these people remain separated from today and fearful of tomorrow. A concerted effort to reach these people is long overdue. They need to be helped back from their islands to the mainland of our concern. But their insular plight is compounded by the fact that they, as well as the rest of us, are also caught up in a sort of split-level syndrome.

People today appear to be suffering from two acute symptoms of a general malaise: separation, which is a cutting away from, and segmenting, which is a cutting up into.

The individual who is having a difficult time finding himself and making decisions will naturally choose the line of least resistance as the easiest one to follow; and this type of person will find it easy to excuse himself by saying, if split-level is the vogue for building today's houses, what's wrong with split loyalties, split personalities, and split-second timing?

And once the process of fragmentation and stratifying begins in the human personality, there is the inevitable pulling away and the pulling apart. And it is precisely for this type of person that the church must have an answer.

Because every Christian is part of the priesthood of believers, each one must, to a large extent, perform his own ministry, searching out the needs that he is best able to meet. But no Christian, however sincere, can make much of an impact on anyone or on any given situation if he has not first formulated some sort of framework for his ministry. But regardless of the specific type of ministry that one may perform best, the overall ministry to the marooned should be prompted by the desire to reassure, to reconcile, and to restore.

The desperate need of human beings for reassurance and reconciliation can be felt at every turn; and because the need is so urgent, even the simplest effort to help can result in a surprising degree of relief and restoration.

I recall a morning several years ago when my youngest child came out of her bedroom and asked me anxiously, "Mommy, do you know that I'm Jennifer?"

Her question was confusing and startling, and for a moment I wondered what she was really asking and what I should answer. But a second glance told me that she had a full-blown case of the mumps. Apparently she had caught her reflection in her dresser mirror and had been shocked by her appearance. With her neck swollen to twice its normal size and her whole face very puffy, it was difficult to recognize herself, and so she had hurried out to see me for reassurance. I was glad to be able to tell her that she would soon be herself.

It didn't take much to relieve my little daughter. Nor does it usually require much more than that to offer relief. It's true that sometimes all we can offer is temporary relief; but at least we can offer that.

Reassurance, reconciliation, and restoration—these are the buoys which keep afloat the lifeline that connects the island to the mainland; these are also the building tools which transform the split-level into a unified whole.

It would seem to me to be a worthwhile experiment for every community of believers to set up a "ministry to the marooned," a concerted effort to reach all separated individuals who have lost touch with God or with their fellowman. The creative impact of such a sustained and dedicated effort is difficult to imagine, but it would surely be well worth the time and energy. The island and the split-level need no longer be the reproachful symbols of an ineffectual Christianity; but the change can only come about when we are willing to take the time that is necessary for a ministry that is based on the principle of "each one reach one."

OUT ON A LIMB

When I was a little girl living in Japan, our family always went to a lake resort for the summer months. I learned to swim at an early age, and each summer I added new skills and new confidence. But the summer I was eleven I had an experience which taught me more than the rudiments of swimming.

There was a tall diving tower with several platforms on it at various levels. One morning I announced to my father that I'd like to swim out to the tower and jump from one of the higher platforms, one which was probably at a height of twenty-five feet. He asked if I really felt ready to try such a jump, and I assured him I was. He offered to swim out to the tower with me and watch.

We climbed up the wet ladder to the level I had chosen. I walked to the edge of the platform, looked down at the water—way, way down—turned around, and headed back to the ladder.

"What are you going to do?" asked my father.

"Climb back down," I explained.

"No, you're not," he corrected. "You said you were coming up here to jump, so that's the way you're going down," he said firmly.

I panicked. I wheedled, I cajoled, I threatened. I staged a first-class tantrum. But nothing availed. Finally, after what seemed like an interminable wait, with my opinion of my father growing more unflattering by the minute, I came to the conclusion that my father's mind was not to be changed. So I jumped. My father followed with an enormous splash.

As we swam back to the pier, he said some things that I have never forgotten.

"You learned something important today," he said. "And sooner or later you would have had to learn it. When you've made up your mind to do something, do it. When you've given your word, you have to follow through. There will be times, like today, when you'll discover that you've taken on more than you bargained for. But you can't back down."

The lesson had been a difficult one; but over the years it has proved to be one of my most valuable. Nor have I learned it completely even yet! It is one of those lessons that must be relearned from time to time.

There is so much wasted effort in every segment of life, both in our secular activities and in the life of the church, because people are too prone to back down or back away or back off. It little matters which phrase we use, for all three express the same result: ground lost.

Rather closely akin to the concept of "ground lost" is a new concept that has sprung from the era of the satellite and the manned space flight: the phenomenon known as weightlessness. A great many of us, upon first hearing of this unusual state of being, shrugged it off as preposterous because it seemed to fly in the face of natural law. Only when the first astronauts substantiated the reality of the theory were we ready to believe it. But in our willingness to accept the fact that the body can, indeed, experience weightlessness, we have made the mistake of trying to transfer this principle into other portions of our lives.

All too often, in our associations with other people, we who claim to be a part of the Christian fellowship are little more than weightless witnesses. All too quickly we back away from the real challenges of our faith whenever these challenges become inconvenient or unpalatable to us. And when a substantial number of Christians back away from their convictions, the whole church loses ground.

We need to be reminded often of the fact that Christ's word carried weight in a time when a man's word counted for little. But why was his word different from that of other men? Might it not have been because he refused to back away? When he said something, it held.

In what records we have of Christ's life, we find example after example of those lonely moments when he refused to retreat. There were the temptations during the forty days in the wilderness when, again and again, he had to say "No!" We remember his reply to those who tried to trick him,

"Render unto Caesar. . . ." We look with awe at the firmness of purpose that set his face toward Jerusalem, though he knew full well what awaited him there. And we cannot help but marvel at his steadfastness in Gethsemane. Nor can we ever forget that even on the cross, when there was still a chance to save himself (and he had the power to have done so), he refused to abdicate his sonship by backing away from the moment of sacrifice. At point after point, throughout his ministry, Christ was offered the chance to retreat. The fact that he did not has made all the difference in the history of mankind!

A contemporary poet, Jane Merchant, has very aptly expressed this basic idea in the second verse of her poem, "The Tall Young Men":

False standards, small examples are not few—
"To get ahead these days you have to cheat."
"Whatever you can get by with is right."
Oh, may we have the strength to be and do
Our best, that, unbewildered by deceit,
The tall young men may live up to their height.

Over and over we see that if a Christian is to touch the sky, he must stand on tiptoe, or sometimes even climb way out on a limb —and perhaps lose his life, to find it!

THE BUTTON

I had heard, over and over again, that God works in strange ways to perform his wonders. I had accepted the fact that it was probably so; but nothing really startling had ever happened to me.

Isn't it odd that the minute we say, "Nothing exciting ever happens to me," it does?

I had been asked to serve as a judge in the dramatic declamatory division of the district speech contest. I sat through a most interesting day, although a tiring one, for I had listened to thirty-four declamations.

They had all been done quite well, but there was one that stood head and shoulders above the rest. It was a story called "The Button," and it had been given in a most gripping fashion by a high school boy who seemed to be living the story as he told it.

The plot revolved around a convict who was in solitary confinement. In order to keep his sanity, he devised a game which he played with a button that had dropped off his shirt. He would throw the button up, listen to see if he could tell where it had dropped in his cell, and then grope around in the darkness until he found it. Then he would repeat the process. But one time when he threw the button up, he didn't hear it come down, and something inside him snapped; he went out of his mind when the one thing he had thought he could depend on disappeared into thin air.

The prison doctor, in making his report to the warden, said he couldn't understand what might have happened. There was nothing in the cell to account for the sudden change in the convict, except—except a spider web in one corner. "And there was a little white button in the middle of it—odd, wasn't it?" mused the doctor.

The contestant who gave this particular

reading received a "One" rating from all three of us who were judging in that section of the contest. He had done a superb job.

Three weeks after the contest I went to a club meeting in a town some thirty-five or forty miles from my home. I had been asked to give a talk on a topic of my own choosing; so I had decided to begin my message with the story of "The Button." It had something to say to all of us, I felt. For we, too, are prone to go to pieces when things don't work out the way we had expected them to; and all of us need some inner resources to hold us steady at those times when life seems to fall apart.

My youngest child accompanied me to the meeting; but there had been so many unexpected events in the last half hour before we left the house that we were late getting started. We finally arrived at the junction of the highway and the town's main street at two minutes before the time the program was to begin.

Not knowing where the meeting hall was and seeing a woman walking down the street, I asked my little girl to roll the window down so that I could ask for directions. However, having just wakened from a catnap, she fumbled sleepily with the window lever just long enough that by the time she rolled the window down the woman had already turned the corner.

I looked hastily out of my window to see if there was anyone coming on that side. I spotted a young fellow standing on the opposite corner, waiting for me to go by so that he could cross the street. I rolled down my window and called out to him.

He came over toward the car to give me the directions I needed; and as he began to talk, I knew I had seen him before, somewhere. And then I placed him.

" 'The Button'—you did 'The Button'!" I exclaimed. He acknowledged that he had. Then I told him what a coincidence it was that I should meet him, for I was going to begin my talk that evening with a synopsis of his declamation. His expression was one of unmasked pleasure and surprise.

Before pulling away from the curb, I wished the boy well in the state competition for which he was now eligible and told him again how impressed I had been with his performance at the district contest.

At the club meeting I not only gave a summary of the story of "The Button," but I mentioned the coincidence of meeting the very boy who had given it. I hadn't remembered his name, nor had I known what town he was from; but suddenly the whole set of circumstances seemed very unusual.

During the coffee hour, which followed the program, a number of women spoke to me about the boy. They told me his name and a great deal about him. He was a person who had never been able to make a success of anything; so everyone in town had been very much surprised when he entered the speech contest—something he had never done before—and they were really surprised when he came back with three "One" ratings.

"Your compliment to him was probably the first encouraging word he has had in years," said one woman.

Suddenly my heart went out to this boy, and I had an overwhelming feeling that I should follow up on him. It seemed like more than a coincidence that our paths should have crossed again.

A few days before the state contest, I wrote the boy a letter wishing him well. Again I commended him on his splendid performance at the district competition. And then I inquired what plans he might have for his future.

I could scarcely wait to find out the results of the state competition. But a few days later I received a letter from the boy, telling me the happy news that he had received all "One" ratings from the judges at the state meet. And then he mentioned that until my letter came he had pretty much decided against going to the state contest. He had been afraid of doing poorly in the larger competition, after having achieved something worthwhile for the first time in his life in the district contest.

He closed his letter by saying, "You asked me what my plans were for the future. I guess I had never thought about it before. But maybe I'd better."

His path and mine have crossed many times since; and each time I feel deeply grateful—grateful that for once I had been sensitive enough to think that perhaps God could use me to help him open the door for somebody. I couldn't help wondering, though, how many other doors had remained closed, that might have been opened if I had been listening.

Every life touches other lives. Each of us has an influence on the lives around us. But how much more meaningful that influence might be if we ourselves could first feel the influence of God. What a pity that most of the time we go our headlong way, scarcely listening, hardly seeing, and wondering why nothing exciting ever seems to happen to us.

NEVERTHELESS

Words are wands which we wave about, and sometimes irresponsibly, to mesmerize the people around us; yet how seldom we use words to work the magic we need for ourselves. Words are pictures, symbols, and once in a while the last vestige of hope to which a human heart can cling.

There is a great proliferation of words, some of them more magical than others, which change the complexion of a situation, transform attitudes, divert, alleviate, enliven, and perform all kinds of remarkable tasks for us.

One word may serve as a balance wheel or perhaps a beacon light; another may be a tightrope; still another becomes a battering ram, and yet another may be a derrick. Words are indeed versatile, and there is one to fit every need.

One of the most valuable words I know—and one for which I am deeply grateful—is "nevertheless." It is a redemptive word, a bridge word. The lifeline from despair to hope is woven with "nevertheless" and with its abbreviated synonym, "but"; and how eagerly we reach for these two words.

Johnny got a D in arithmetic this time; *nevertheless*, he did keep his B in spelling.

Your train just pulled out, sir, *but* there's a bus leaving in ten minutes that'll get you there at about the same time.

The electricity's off, *but* isn't it fun to eat by candlelight!

Janie spilled her milk; *nevertheless*, be thankful it wasn't grape juice on this white tablecloth!

After turning this matter over in our minds a bit, we might well ask a leading question. Wouldn't it be reassuring and heartwarming if we could transmit to our children the ability to look at life from a "nevertheless" point of view? How much more enduring a gift like that would be than most of the expensive gifts we offer!

A generation that has come to regard as commonplace such superlatives as "spectacular" and "colossal" and "king-size" will need something sturdy, rather than superlative, to satisfy the verbal void. People who are glib about the spectacular are eventually going to feel colossal dissatisfaction with life as they are seeing it. And in the low spots, when life is deglamorized, despair can grow to be king-size.

What can be done with despair? Is there not some sure way out of it? Perhaps one of the more hopeful directions away from the downdraft lies over the bridge of "nevertheless." And we may take even more heart in the knowledge that very early in his life, Jesus discovered this vital bridge. The discovery was a natural and inevitable one for him.

Christ was a builder. His boyhood years in the carpenter shop had taught him the use of hammer, saw, and chisel. He knew well the textures of the wood with which he worked; he could distinguish quickly between the hardwoods and the soft. He understood perfecctly the importance of symmetry and design, and he appreciated the contrasting patterns in the grain of the wood. However, it was not only the beauty of the wood that concerned him. For in a land where life was difficult, things had to have a purpose.

But by the very fact that life was hard, people's hopes and purposes frequently faltered. Christ, being a master craftsman, understood the frailty of the lives with which he worked. He saw their weaknesses, their shallowness, their cowardice. *Nevertheless,* he forgave them, and he loved them.

Ten lepers had been healed; only one returned to thank him for his gift of healing. The other nine went their heedless way, apparently utterly lacking in gratitude; but Christ did not take back the gift he had given, nor did he begrudge them their newfound joy. Insensitive and self-centered, the nine lepers were totally unaware that "nevertheless" was the bridge of forgiveness that Christ built for them.

When Christ gathered with his disciples in the upper room, he took the basin and the towel and washed the disciples' feet. This was a startling reversal of the accepted order of things. It was the disciples who should have been serving their Lord; *nevertheless,* he knew that only by acting what he had been preaching could he convey the concept of the true servant and the true master. "Nevertheless" was the bridge of service over which he crossed into the lives of his friends there in the upper room.

Then there was the experience in the Garden of Gethsemane, when the disciples fell asleep after he had asked them to watch and pray. There is no doubt that this was deeply disappointing to Him; *nevertheless,* he understood that although the spirit is usually willing, too often the flesh is weak. And so with keen compassion he bridged the chasm of alienation.

Then, soon after this discouraging incident, Peter, who had pledged his unwavering loyalty, betrayed his Lord—and betrayed him not once but three times! *Nevertheless,* Christ was willing to build his church on the truth Peter grasped concerning his identity. "Nevertheless" became the bridge of trust which, when men crossed over it, could make them tall.

In that fateful Garden of Gethsemane, Christ had prayed from out of the deep torment of his soul, "If it be possible, let this cup pass from me; *nevertheless,* not as I will, but as thou wilt."

"Nevertheless" was the bridge of obedience over which Christ knew he must walk if he was to cross over from the human to the divine. In Gethsemane, Christ faced what was perhaps his most difficult "nevertheless."

The skeptic will say, as he always has, "It may be true that Christ prayed such a prayer as that—and we have to admire him for it—nevertheless, we mustn't forget that in spite of his goodness, he was put to death."

But the believer will answer confidently, "*Nevertheless*, he rose from the dead!" And through his resurrection he gave us freely and triumphantly a bridge to eternal life.

FAITH IS A FLOTILLA

I have some extraordinarily happy memories of my childhood and particularly of my summers as a small child. The long, lazy days of July and August were always spent at a charming lake that was ringed by a circle of cozy hills.

The memories of those summers in Japan are myriad, and they all seem to be inextricably connected with the lake itself and the experiences that were related to it.

Brightly etched on the tablet of my heart is the remembrance of Sunday evenings at Lake Nojiri. There was a tradition which was developed over the years of holding a hymn sing on the lake every Sunday evening when the weather would permit.

Just about dusk the largest sailboat on the lake would go out near the middle of the lake and lower her sails. She would drop anchor and wait there for the other boats to arrive. Bit by bit, as the soft gray of the sky turned into a velvet blackness, the other boats would push off from shore, dozens of them: rowboats, sampans, canoes, rafts, anything that would float. The first little boats arriving at the big sailboat would cluster around it; the next arrivals would form a second ring around the first ring of boats; and so the circles grew until in less than half an hour there was a veritable flotilla in the middle of the lake.

The central sailboat carried a small portable organ, and the music began as soon as there were enough people clustered around the boat to "make a joyful noise." We sang and sang, often for as long as two hours. There was never a sermon; somehow it didn't seem necessary out there where the stars twinkled a million sermons. And it was seldom that we had any formal prayers at this vesper service. The entire experience was a prayer.

Each little boat had a brightly decorated Japanese lantern at its bow and stern. These helped us to see the words of the hymns—although we came to know most of them by heart—but the lanterns also served another purpose. They were friendly reminders to all who saw them from the shore that out there—in the middle of the lake—was a community of faith, a group of singing Christians, a fellowship of light. Some who watched from the shore were already believers; some were skeptics or scoffers; a few had yet to hear of the Light of the world; but to all, the light on the lake was a bright proclamation that the darkness cannot overcome the light.

The closing hymn at every one of those vesper services was always the same, bringing to every heart a marvelous quiet and healing. And an indescribable sense of peace and well-being settled over us as we sang the third verse of the poem that was so beautifully written by Whittier and set to music by Frederick Maker:

O sabbath rest by Galilee!
O calm of hills above,
Where Jesus knelt to share with thee

The silence of eternity,
Interpreted by love!

In remembering the lovely tradition at Lake Nojiri, I feel that it may not be too farfetched to think of the Christian churches as a great flotilla. At the center—the anchor and the source of the music—is Christ. Gathered around him are Christians of every hue, of varying persuasions and practices; and each of them carries a light, a small light symbolic of the greater flame, the Light of the world.

There is water everywhere, and it is deep—and troubled. But the flotilla does not fear, for it is linked together; and it is strong, because it has a center. The song is a glad one as the flotilla spreads its light against the darkness.

THE NEED FOR A DECIDUOUS FAITH

Having lived many of my years in New England, I came to have a deep and abiding appreciation of trees. New England's hills are famous for their fall foliage, but they are magnificent any time of year. The profusion of pine forests laced with the incredible white of the birches created a splendor that stirred the heart. And then, when the red of the maples ate like a fire across the hills, the heart could scarcely bear so much beauty. There were days in October when it was almost painful to look out upon such a vast loveliness; but November brought relief, when the final bright leaf had fallen.

The falling of the leaves brought to the New Englander a certain kind of salvation, for he could not possibly have survived two months of October.

True, there is a sadness that accompanies the shedding of the foliage on those crisp autumn days, when the smell of wood smoke adds to this vague feeling of sorrow. But the loss of the leaves is a necessary part of growing and replenishing the forests, and so we let them go—one by one, the crimson and the gold.

Trees, from the beginning of time, have whispered their secrets to man; and he, learning the lessons of the deep woods, has planted the knowledge in his heart.

Deeply implanted in man's heart is his awareness that he is part of a remarkable creation; and his faith, nurtured by this knowledge, sends its roots down into the very depths of his being. And because the roots go deep, he is afraid to shake the maple of his faith, lest some of the leaves should fall. But it is necessary that this be done, to make room for the new growth that will come on in the spring.

Man—Christian man—must insist on a deciduous faith, one that can shed the faded leaves of old platitudes, to make way for the sprouting of new buds of belief.

This is, in fact, a deciduous age in which we live. Whole systems of thought are discarded without the blinking of an eye; scientific findings become old almost before they leave the test tube; and technological discoveries become obsolete on the drawing board.

To be deciduous is to discard, not destroy. To shake the brittle leaves from the tree is different from felling the tree. A deciduous faith, then, is one that is willing to discard the ideas that are no longer tenable; but this does not mean that it destroys the tree of belief itself.

The concept of deciduousness is certainly not new. Jesus introduced it in his story about putting new patches on old cloth and his parable about the new wine in old wineskins. His entire message underscored the need for ridding ourselves of the old encumbrances that hinder our growth as children of God. His ideas were indeed revolutionary for the men of his day; for they wanted to keep the security of old things, no matter how outmoded they may have been. And the men who listened found it difficult to comprehend. Perhaps it was too much to have expected them to grasp the principle of deciduousness, for their frame of reference was the palm tree!

When Christ cleansed the temple of the money changers, he was getting rid of an ancient blight. The tree of the Judaic faith was groaning under the weight of so many layers of leaves, and it was necessary to shake some loose.

When Jesus refused to condemn the woman who was brought before him to be stoned, he shook off one of the cruel encumbrances of the day. And suddenly the woman found that there was still the green sprout of hope that would eventually grow into a new self-respect.

Christ understood very well that there is the time of greening which comes to heal the places on the branches where the former leaves had been.

So is there the time of greening in the heart of man. Despair, like snow, may cover the soul for a season, but it will pass.

The mature Christian must teach the learning Christian what he knows about the seasons of the heart. The promise of the time of greening is sufficient to sustain him through the winter of his doubt. And doubt is not all wrong—for only when the seeker could say, "I believe; help my unbelief," was he able to feel within him the first faint stirring of spring.

Our children, living through this uncertain season, may hesitate to loosen the leaves—there are so few on their tree. But we must sit with them patiently at the foot of the tree and wait with them for the time of greening.

But even in spring there is sometimes a sudden reminder of winter. And we must help them to understand this, too. Our children will someday climb that tree and revel in its fresh green leaves.

One spring night long ago an unexpected blanket of snow covered the earth. The next morning, when my little daughter discovered what had happened, she pressed her happy face against the window and exclaimed ecstatically, "Oooooooooo, it hasn't un-Christmased yet!"

This, then, is the high privilege of us all—to keep life from "un-Christmasing"!

EPILOGUE

It is stern work, it is perilous work, to
thrust your hand in the sun
And pull out a spark of immortal flame
to warm the hearts of men.

—JOYCE KILMER